20 個必學象形漢字練習簿 - 5

20 Must-learn Pictographic Chinese Characters Workbook

5

Coloring, Handwriting, Zhuyin

白雲

20 Must-Learn Pictographic Chinese Characters Workbook 5
Coloring, Handwriting, Zhuyin

Illustrated by Chris Huang
Edited by Iris Chiou
Proof Read by Edith Yuan
Published by Cloud Chinese
All copyrights © by Chuming Huang
Inside 44 pages Black & White
Paperback Color with Matte finished
Printed in US, by KDP
ISBN 13 : 978-1-954729-91-9
Reference ID: 20AmaPap01
Language: : Chinese
Publication Date: 2021, Feb 25th

白雲文化教育

白雲文化以傳承母國文化為目標，出版適合咱海外下一代的繁體注音繪本及教材。

CLOUD LEARNING
www.mycloudchinese.com
myeasyshows@gmail.com

白雲華語學苑
快樂學習的線上華語學校

白雲華語學苑是白雲文化的附屬中文學校，是海外第一家全線上華語僑校。以快樂學習華語、傳承台灣文化、愛家和生活為教學目標。

注音基礎班-各年級（K-12）招生中，歡迎聯絡白雲。

CLOUD CHINESES SCHOOL
www.mycloudchineseschool.com
school@mycloudchinese.com
847-917-0036

TABLE OF CONTENTS

LOOK

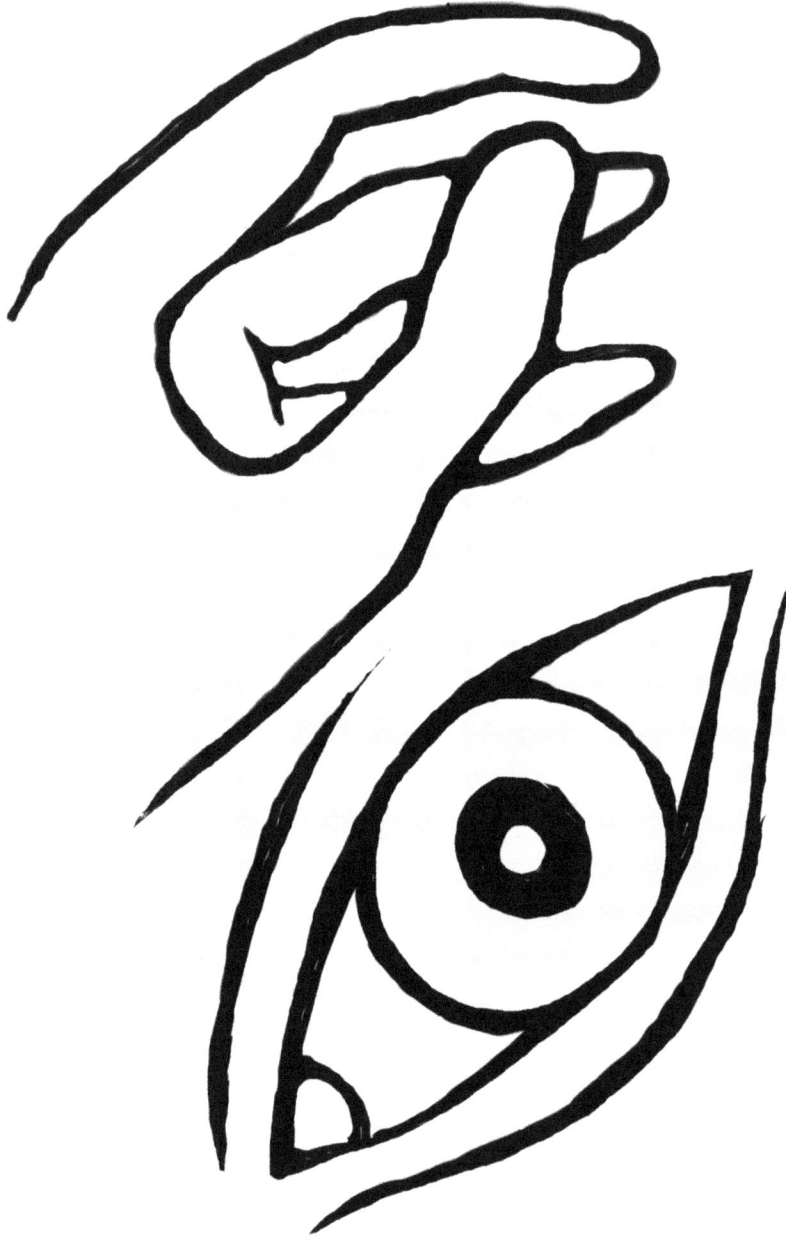

看 ㄎ
ㄢˋ
Kàn

看 ㄎㄢˋ

（一）

看見 ㄎㄢˋ ㄐㄧㄢˋ

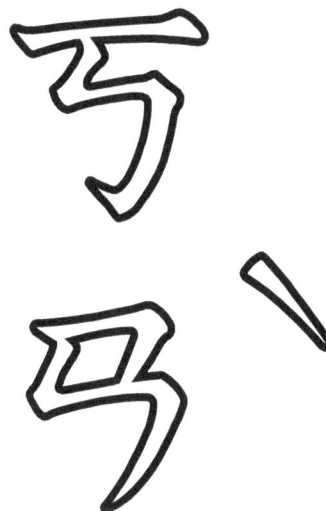
ㄎㄢˋ
ㄎㄢ

SEE

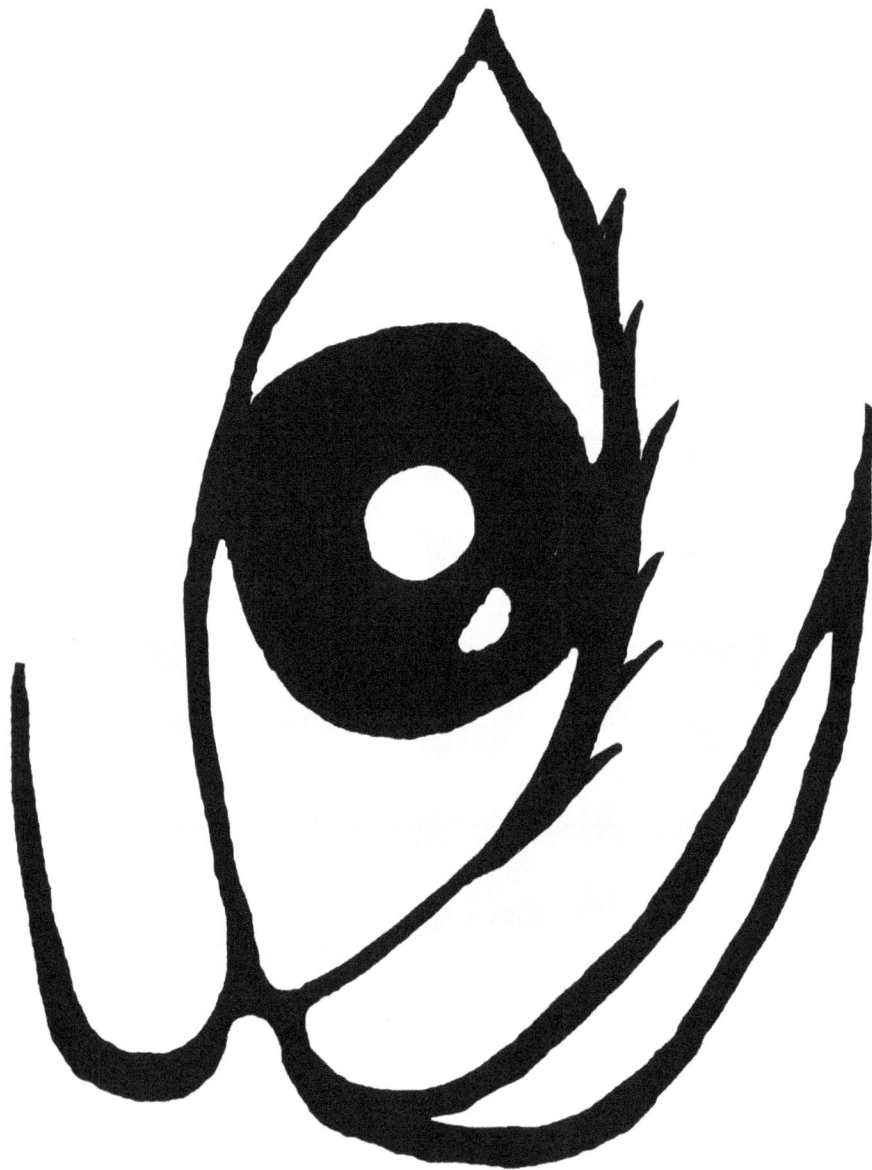

見 ㄐㄧㄢˋ Jiàn

見　ㄐㄧㄢˋ

看見　ㄎㄢˋ　ㄐㄧㄢˋ

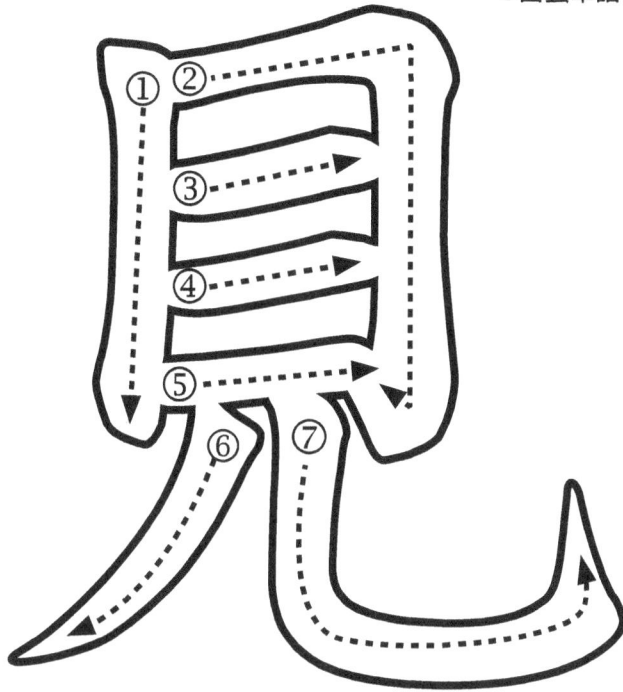

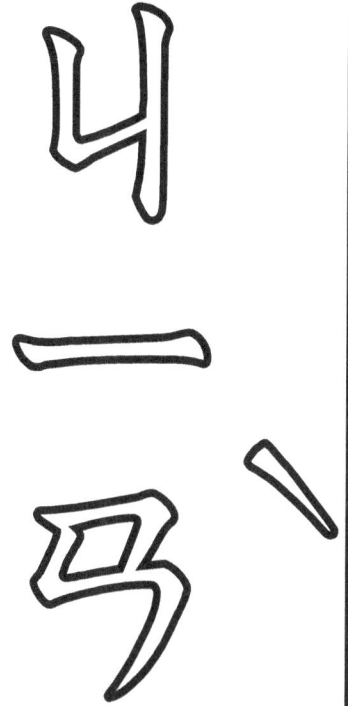

CRY

哭 ㄎ
ㄨ Kū

哭 ㄎㄨ

哭 ㄎㄨ

ㄎ
ㄨ

LAUGH

笑 ㄒㄧㄠˋ Xiào

笑 ㄒㄧㄠˋ

笑 ㄒㄧㄠˋ

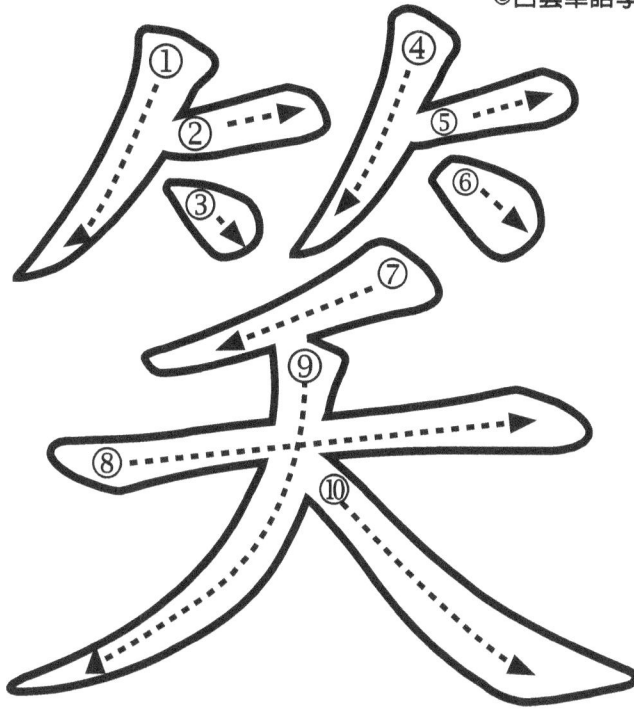

ㄒㄧㄠˋ

CALL

叫 ㄐㄧㄠˋ Jiào

叫 ㄐㄧㄠˋ

叫 ㄐㄧㄠˋ

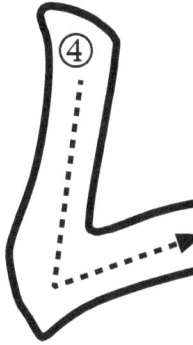

SING

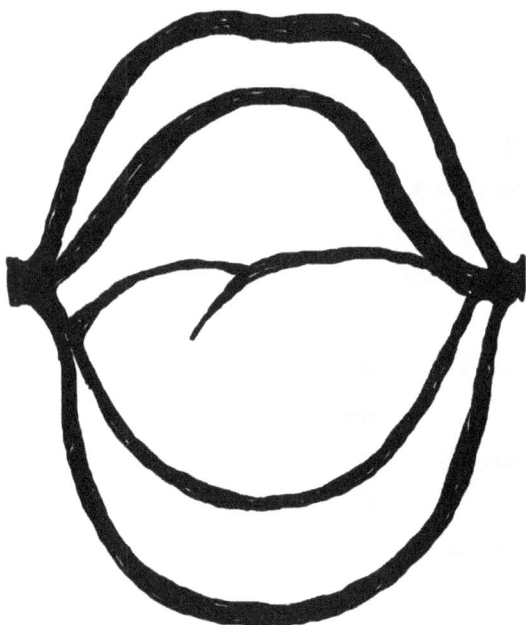

唱 　 ㄔㄤˋ

Chàng

白雲
mycloudchineseschool.com

唱 ㄔㄤˋ

唱 ㄔㄤˋ
歌 ㄍㄜ

ㄔㄤˋ

GO

走 ㄗ
　 ㄡˇ
Zǒu

| 走 | ㄗㄡˇ |

走 ㄗㄡˇ
路 ㄌㄨˋ

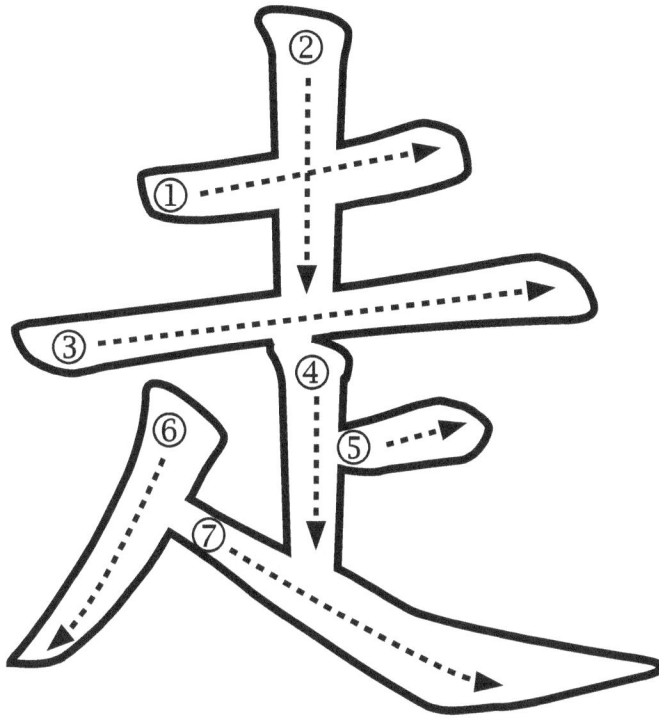

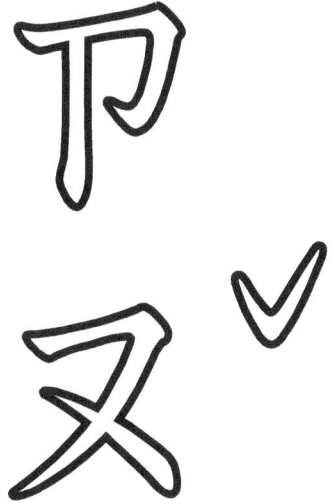

巴 ㄅㄚ Bā

巴 ㄅㄚ

巴 ← 下巴 ㄒㄧㄚˋ·ㄅㄚ

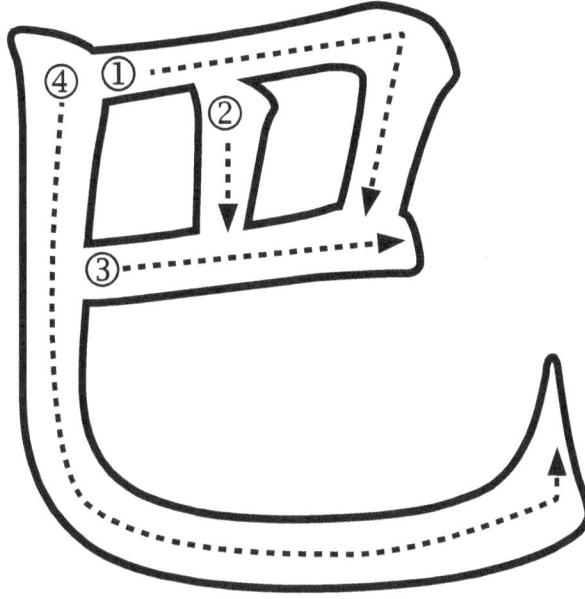

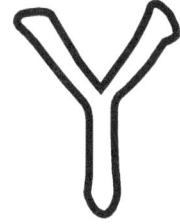

ㄅㄚ

FINISH

了　ㄌ
　　ㄜ　Le

了 ˙ㄌㄜ

了

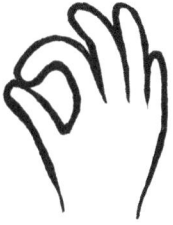

好了 ㄏㄠˇ ˙ㄌㄜ

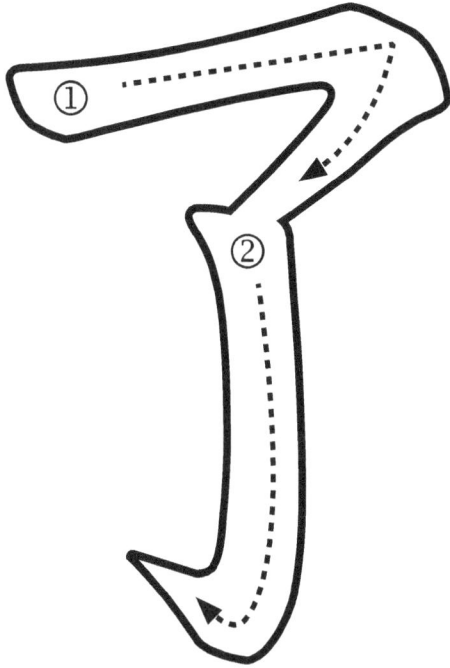

ㄌ

ㄜ

COMPARE

比 ㄅ ˇ
Bǐ

比 ㄅ一ˇ

比較 ㄅ一ˇ ㄐ一ㄠˋ

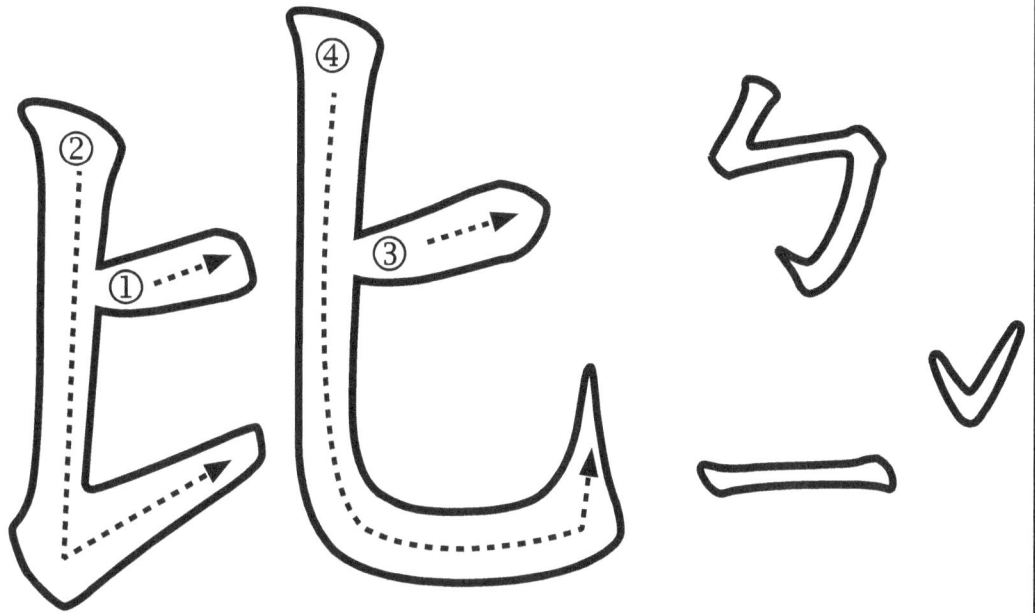

ㄅ一ˇ

PLUM

李 ㄌ
　　一 ˇ
　　　Lǐ

李　ㄌㄧˇ

李子　ㄌㄧˇ ㄗˇ

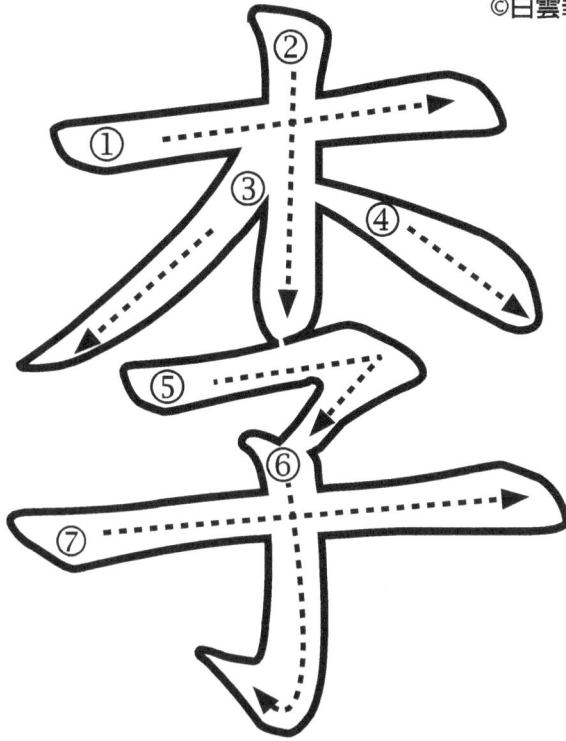

ㄌ
ㄧ ˇ

KNIFE

刀 ㄉ
ㄠ Dāo

刀	ㄉㄠ

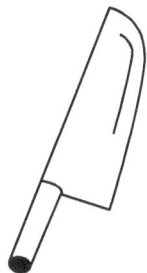

刀子 ㄉㄠ ˙ㄗ

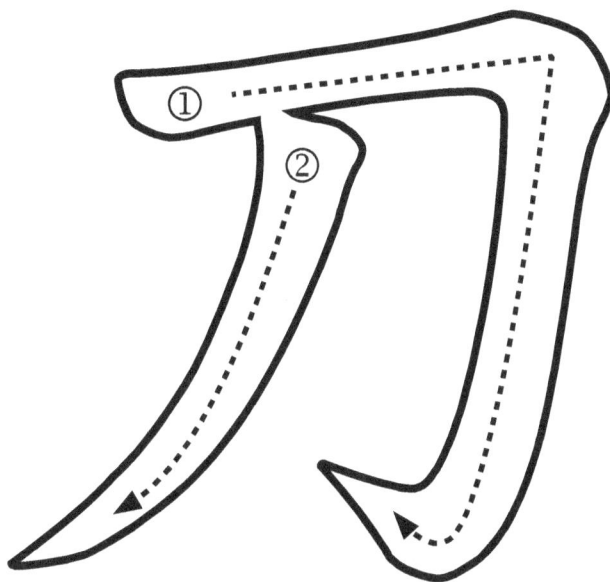

ㄉ
ㄠ

SEAT

位 ㄨㄟˋ
Wèi

位 ㄨㄟˋ

座位
ㄗㄨㄛˋ ㄨㄟˋ

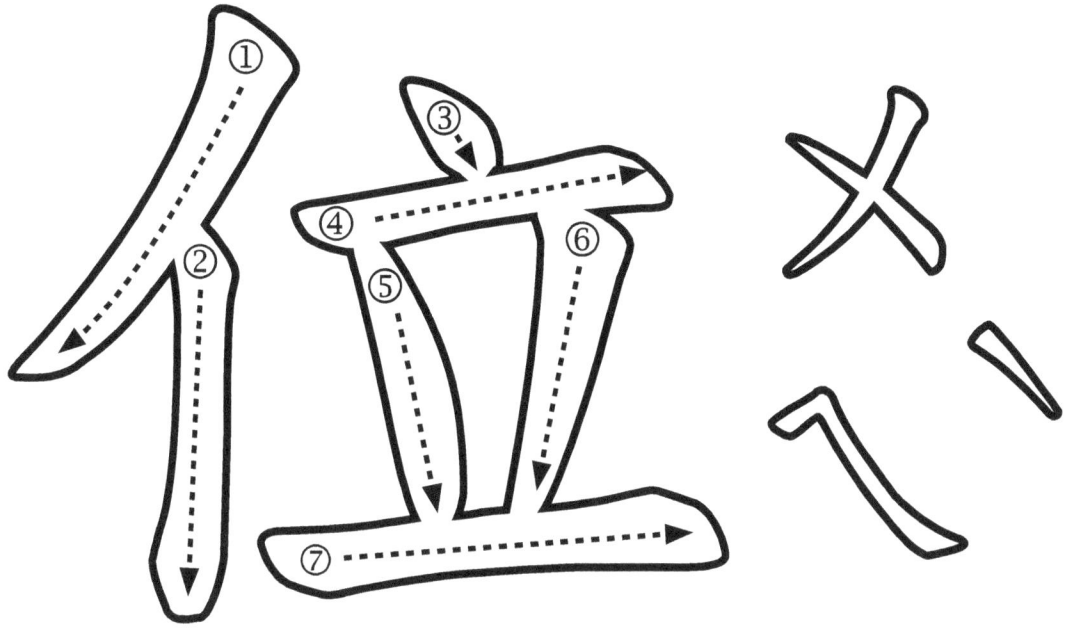

YEAH

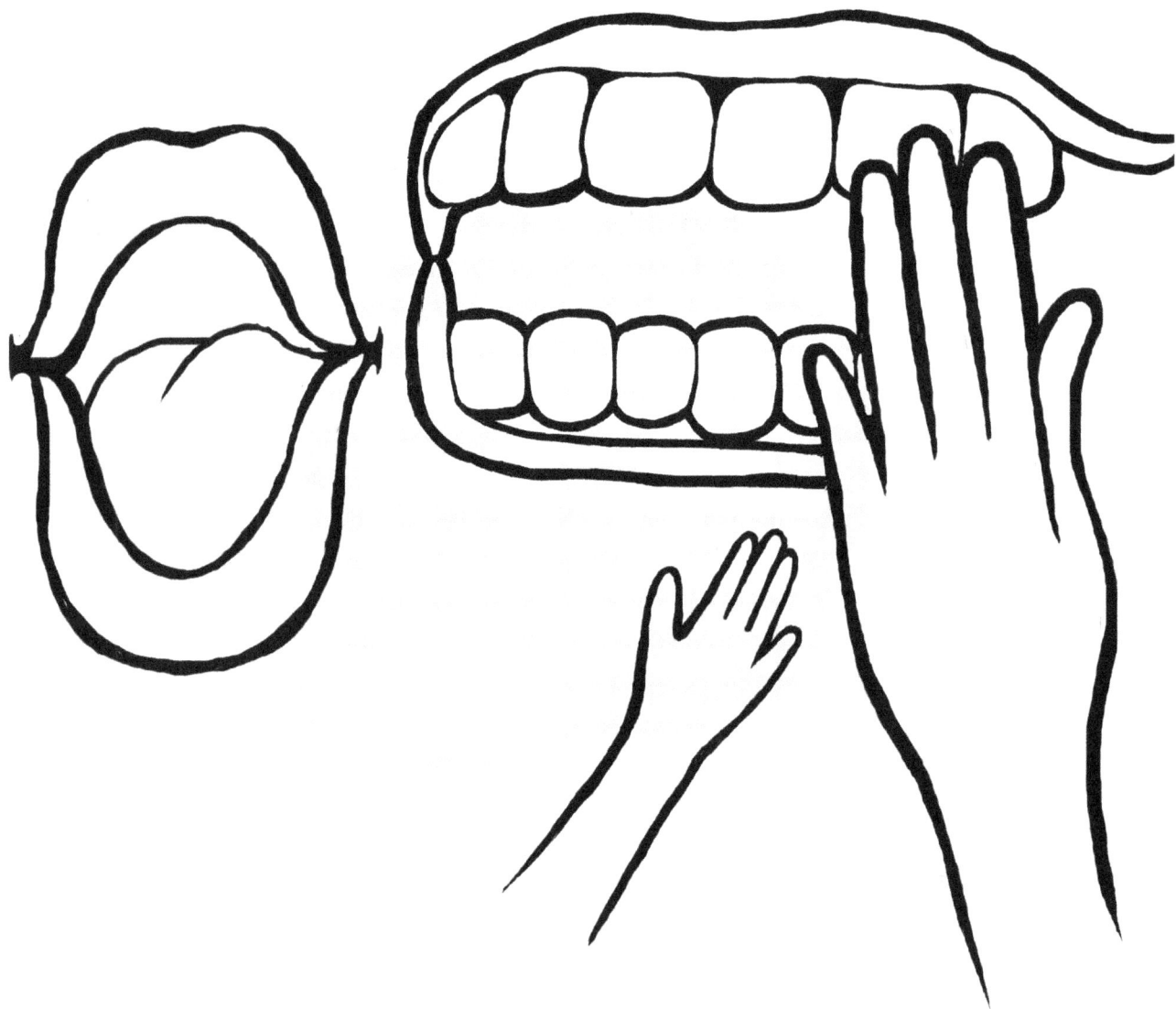

呀 ˙
Y
Ya

呀 ˙ㄧㄚ

好 ㄏㄠˇ
呀 ˙ㄧㄚ

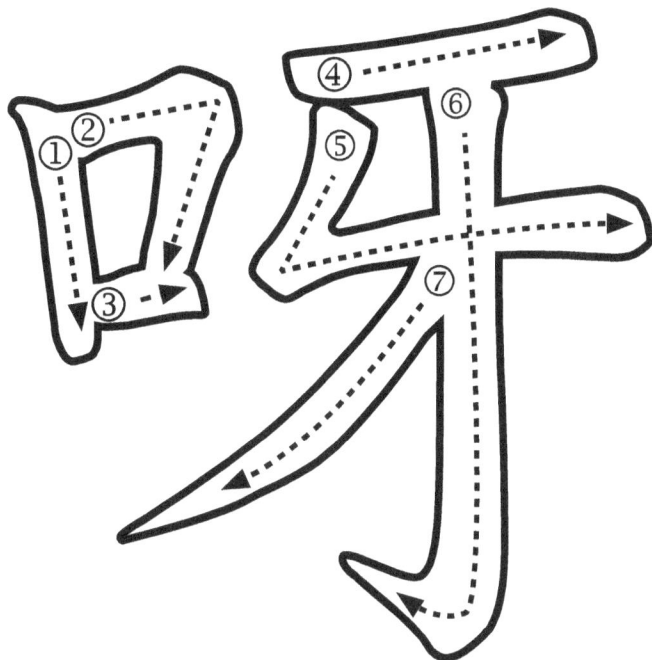

GRASS

草 ㄘ
ㄠˇ
Cǎo

草　ㄘㄠˇ

草　ㄘㄠˇ

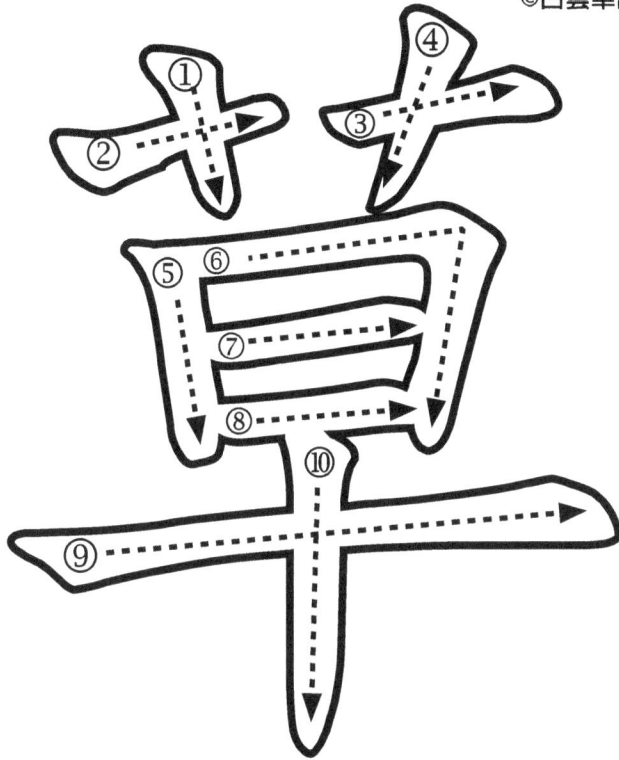

ㄘ
ㄠˇ

ELEPHANT

象 ㄒ一ㄤˋ Xiàng

象 ㄒㄧㄤˋ

大象 ㄉㄚˋ ㄒㄧㄤˋ

ㄒㄧㄤˋ

35

CROSS

交 ㄐㄧㄠ Jiāo

交 ㄐㄧㄠ

Ｘ

交叉 ㄐㄧㄠ ㄔㄚ

ㄐ
ㄧ
ㄠ

FRIEND

朋 ㄆㄥˊ Péng

朋 ㄆㄥˊ

朋 ㄆㄥˊ
友 一ㄡˇ

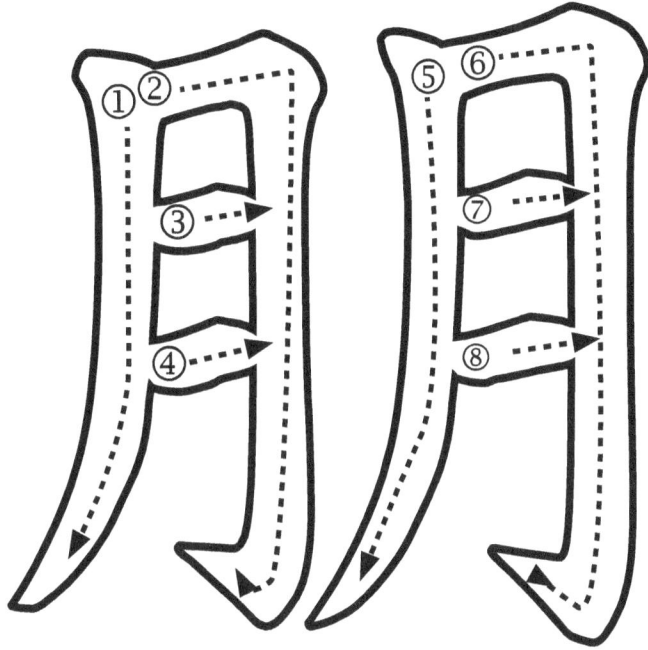

ㄆ
ㄥ
ˊ

FRIEND

友 ㄧㄡˇ
Yǒu

友 ㄧㄡˇ

朋 ㄆㄥˊ
友 ㄧㄡˇ

友 ㄧㄡˇ

quantifier of animals

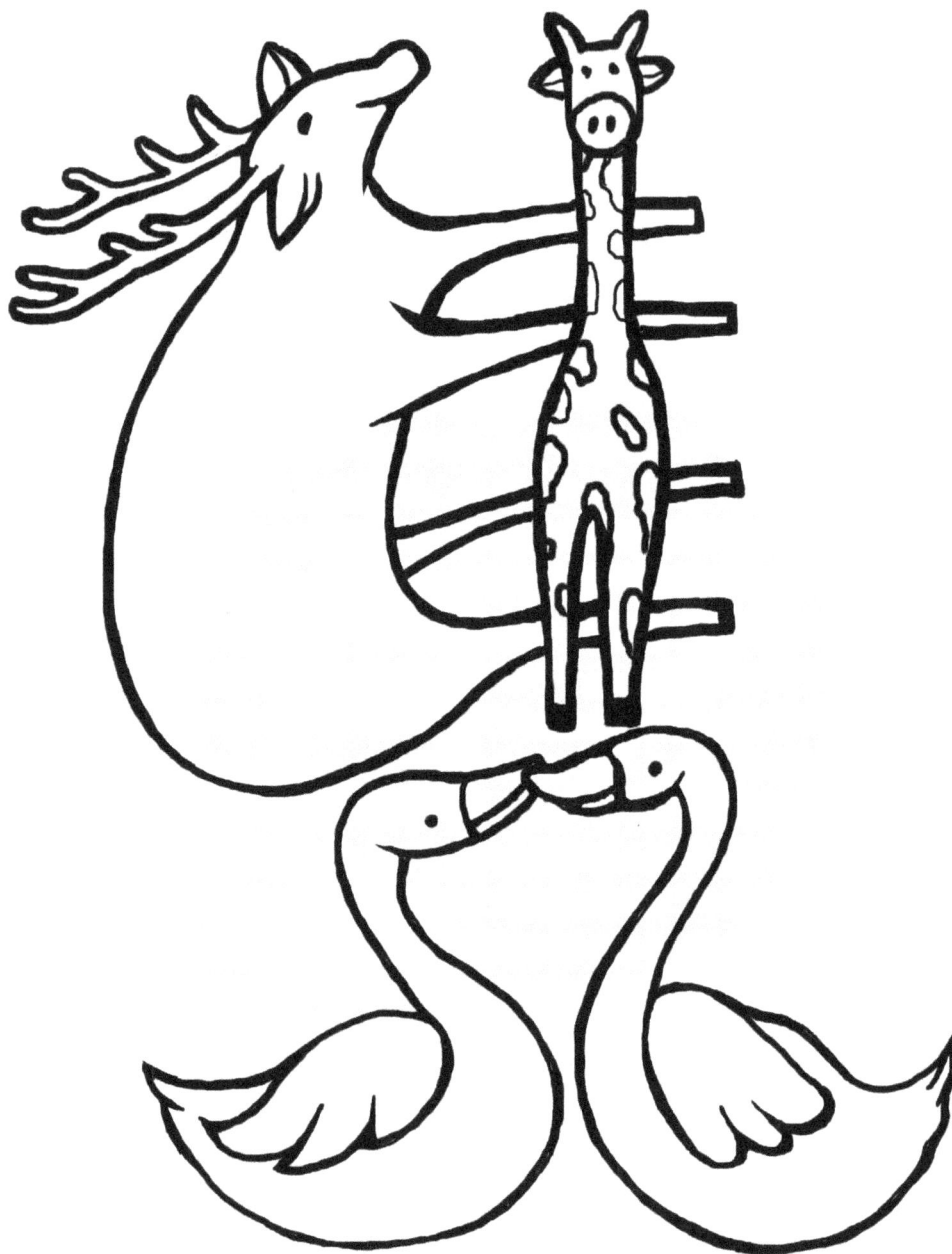

隻 ㄓ

Zhī

隻 ㄓ

一 ㄓ 隻 ㄧ 鴨 ㄚ

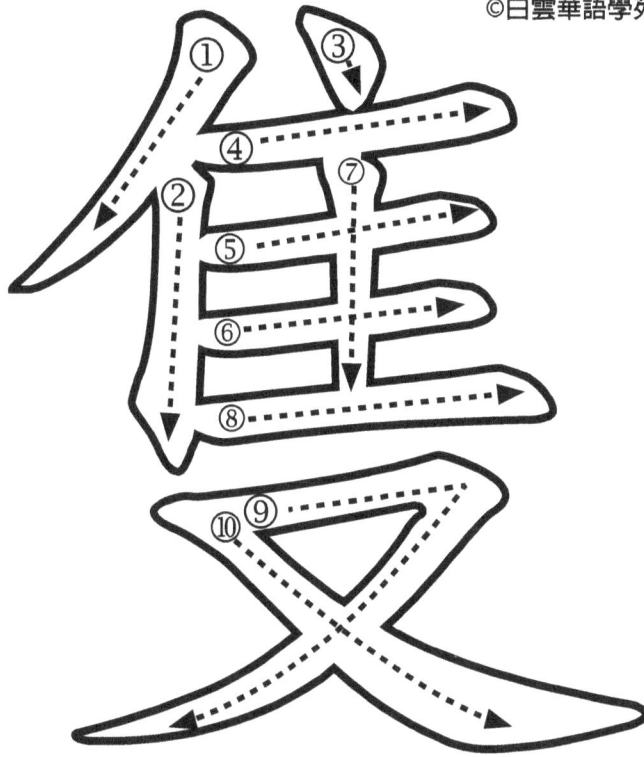

ㄓ

黃老師
Chris Huang
● 主編

白雲團隊編製

EZ說華語
EZ Chinese Conversation

拼音拼讀全集
Chinese Pinyin Pronunciation

說說華語
Our Chinese Conversations

中文數學練習題
Chinese Word Problems Workbook

黃老師
Chris Huang
● 繪圖
● 編寫

阿嬤的滷肉飯
Ama's Lu Rou Fan

媽媽的家在台灣
Mama's Home in Taiwan

我愛媽媽
I Love Mama

Yummy 100

我的ㄅㄆㄇ練習本
My Zhuyin Workbook

我的說唱畫ㄅㄆㄇ讀本
My Zhuyin RAP & Drawing

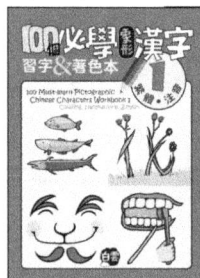

100個必學象形漢字
100 Must-learn Pictographic Chinese

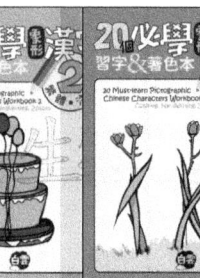

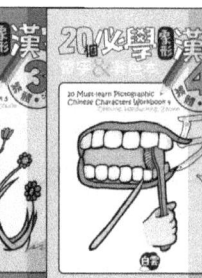

www.ingramcontent.com/pod-product-compliance
Lightning Source LLC
Chambersburg PA
CBHW081242020426
42331CB00013B/3274